Ship of Thougnts

Mranali Joshi

BookLeaf Publishing

India | USA | UK

Presentation by *BookLeaf Publishing*

Web: www.bookleafpub.com

E-mail: info@bookleafpub.com

ISBN: 9789363315068

First edition 2024

*For my mother, who doesn't believe in
half-measures,*

For my father, who always believes in me.

ACKNOWLEDGEMENT

They lie if they believe that writing is a lonely profession. Many people and places in Mother Nature encourage me to weave my thoughts into poems. And I would like to thank them.

I would like to thank my brother Dronesh Joshi for his ideology and support. I thank my friends who motivate me to jot down my thoughts into words and my words into poetry.

I also thank BookLeaf Publishing for showing a keen interest in publishing my rhythmic record.

Indore
July 2024
Mranali Joshi

PREFACE

"In the quiet interplay of the ink and emotions, these poems emerge as whispers of the thoughts, each poem is a testament to the profound connections we forge with ourselves and the world around us."

As I reflect on the journey of crafting these poems, I'm reminded of moments of solitude and introspection that have shaped my thoughts, and my perspective towards life and art.

Throughout *Ship of Thoughts*, you will encounter recurring motifs of nature's beauty, the complexities of human relationships, understanding, bonding, and the quest for inner peace amidst turmoil.

Each poem in this collection emerged from a place of deep emotion and contemplation. I sought to capture fleeting moments and emotions in words, striving for clarity and authenticity in every line.

Through this book, I aim to pen down my experiences, imagination, my journey till now, and something that has happened to me or to my friends and family. With this book I tried to create verses that not only speak to the heart but also invite readers to reflect on their own experiences.

Thank you, dear readers, for embarking on this poetic journey with me. May *Ship of Thoughts*, resonate with you and offer moments of solace and reflection in your own lines.

Once upon a time

There was a girl, once upon a time,
Wakes up before the sun shines,
With laughter that danced like wind chimes,
Her eyes held dreams of mountains to climb,
Choose to have chia seeds with honey and lime,
From traditional attire to modern design,
Love to travel with friends and family but solo
most of the time,
Answered all *ifs* and *buts* and decided to stay
where moonbeams align,
Getting older but fine like wine,
Hence, there was a girl, once upon a time.

An Evening in Paris

An evening in Paris, invokes a sense of romance
and elegance,
Where dreams are woven in lace,
Where history whispers at every place,
Where art galleries showcase masterpieces,
Where the timeless art "Eiffel Tower" embraces,

The sound of distant melodious music playing in
cafès,
A candlelit dinner at a cost bistro, savoring fine
wine and delicious French pastries,
Where theaters commence performances from
classical ballets to contemporary plays,

In every corner and street, a story to be found,
A city full of surprises, endlessly profound,
Oh Paris, in your lightweight dance and sway,
Eternally in love with you, night and day.

Unplanned Journey

It happens, when you take unplanned turns,
usually it calls to go with the flow and cut the
thorns,

In the quiet corners of a strolling mind,
A journey unpack, unforeseen, undefined,

No map in hand, no compass to guide right,
only the light in day and silence in the night,

Through the deep valley and mountains high,
build the castle by the sea and let soul fly,

So wander on, with spirit bold,
In the tale of journey, yet untold...

Sit with it

Sit with it, even though you want to run,
Sit with it, even though you don't want to face,
Sit with it, even when it's heavy and difficult to
accept,
Sit with it, even though you're not quite sure of
the way through,
Sit with it, even though you're in ache and pain,
Let tears fall like gentle rain,
Embrace the shadows, the fear that clings,
As you wait for the dawn that morning will
bring,
Sit with it, in love's warm glow,
Engage in bonds that grow,
Let happiness bloom, like flowers in spring,
In every breath, in every living thing,
Sit with it, because this too shall pass,
A delicate moment, like shards of glass..

Brown Eyes

Brown and bold,
The nights were cold,
Tons of secrets to be told,

Yet rich and deep,
Unloved, free, and asleep,
Sometimes full of tears, weep,

In the pool of warmth, the earthy hue,
Reflecting stories old and new,

A depth that hides no pain,
No hope, no loss, no gain,

Never underestimate the brown eyes,
For they can bring you down to your knees.

Being Selfish

It's not wrong being selfish, if it's for your
health,
To care for oneself is not a crime,
To seek one's path in the sand of time,

Be selfish when you want to listen to your heart,
To cherish your dreams and to fulfill desires,
Be selfish before it's too late and you retire,

Be selfish when it's about your mental peace and
harmony,
Do remember you are not everyone's cup of tea.

So let's embrace this selfish grace,
To carve your destiny, to weave your thoughts,
to find your place.

If not now then when

Get up and start, if not now then when,
Before the time flies and nothing's left in hand,

In the silence of morning's light,
Birds chirping, thoughts are taking flight,

The moments slip like grains of sand,
Through fingers held, yet never planned,

In quiet corners of the mind,
Don't let regrets echo in ears and bind,

The heart beats out a steady rhyme,
Yearning for its chosen time,

To leap beyond the bounds of fear,
Find what's true, what's pure and what's near,

Paint the canvas of our days, seize the moment
my friend,
Live fullest, do the due as planned,
Get up and start, if not now then when?...

There is nothing wrong

There is nothing wrong with being born black,
There is nothing wrong with walking on the
wrong track,

There is nothing wrong with moments full of
doubt,
They teach us lessons we can't live without,

Nothing wrong if you fall for someone again,
Earn it, grab it, repeat it again,

There is nothing wrong if you feel attracted
towards,
Feel free, move ahead, don't look backwards,

There is nothing wrong with shedding tears,
Letting emotions flow, releasing fear,

There is nothing wrong to go away and
disappear,
If you feel unwanted, abandoned, not near..........

Salary Day

Another buck,
Another day,
My hard-earned money spent,
But the tax and expenses are paid.

The work is tough
And the pay is low,
But that is just
The way life goes.

We sacrifice
Nearly 70% of our lives
To make money and to make ends meet
And stay alive.

So, take it slow
And enjoy the roller coaster ride
'Cause you never know
The day, the moment, at the end you gonna
die.....

Distinct yet together

He scrolls the news,
While she reads the books,
She likes the mountains,
He craves the sea.

She is an early bird,
He is a night owl,
He loves the seafood,
She is a lacto-vegetarian.

He'd rather drive,
She mostly takes the plane,
He waits for sunshine,
She walks in the rain.

He gulps down chilled beer,
She sips hot coffee,
He asks, "Why go?"
She says, "Why not?"

Mostly they disagree on everything,
Still respect each other's decision....
Yes, they exist..

You Should If You Could

Isn't it better to paint a picture and write a letter?
To compose your own lyrics or click some
random pics,
To bake a cake or plant a seed,
Think over the difference between want and
need.

You should if you could, remember there is not
much time,
With rivers to swim and mountains to climb,

Books to read and music to hear,
If confused, don't worry, start with Shakespeare.

Get up, start up, the world is waiting out there,
With sunshine in your eyes, and wind blowing
your hair,

A fall of snow, a shower of rain,
Seize the day, this will not come round again.

You should if you could, but bear in mind,
Old age will come surely and it won't be that
kind,

Thus, travel, explore, meet the newbie,
You should, you could, before you die.

Remember

Walls have ears,
Doors have eyes,
When it's not worth,
Stop being nice.

Embrace the rain,
Forget the worry and the pain,
Cherish the snow,
Sip the coffee whenever you feel low.

Beware of people,
Who have eyes like eagle,
They wear masks and differently glow,
And you think, you very well know.

RIP Bad Day

Birds still sing,
Sun still shines,
The sea is calling,
And mountains to climb,
Just rip the bad day,
It may be yours,
Or may be mine.

Ten

If I met my ten-year-old self today,
What would I tell her,
What would I say?
Would I warn her of the future,
Of the bad or worse things yet to come?
Or would I leave her be, simple & naive,
To keep having fun?
'Cause my Ten-year-old-self believed the
world was a perfect place to live in,
Would she recognise herself, if she
looked into my face?
Even though my journey till now was not
that easy, I have learnt much more,
Twenty years have passed since then,
I would give up everything I have,
To view, to live, to weave life
through her eyes again,
If I get a chance, will live my life as ten again..

Yours and Mine

Life is yours, death is mine,
Peace is yours, stress is mine,
Happiness is yours, sorrow is mine
Everything is yours & yours everything is mine.

Temporary People

You meet many people in your journey,
Some are egoistic and few are worthy,

Some were only meant for dreams and laughter,
They only stay till the weather changes and
quickly disappear,

Then come the ones who are meant for forever,
Always supporting behind the mirror,

They were cast in iron and set in gold,
And never leave you even after you become
bold and old,

Know the worth of those people,
No matter how difficult or typical,

Not everyone in your life is temporary,
Couple of them are necessary and legendary.

One for Fearless Women

She is the writer of her own story,
Shining through the world, turning history into
her story,

Defined by no man, fighting all alone,
Paying all her bills and all her loan,

Sometimes traditional, sometimes liberal,
At times novel and more practical,

She is both — sometimes prayer, sometimes
war,
Don't try to catch her; she seems near but is
so-so-so far.

Doors to Mountain

At the base of Himalayan peaks where shadows
fall,
There is a door to mountain, still and tall.

Created by nature, somewhere alone, somewhere
with the sea face,
Guardians of secrets in a timeless space.

A journey of spirit, where dreams reside,
Soaring peaks, remote locations, and majestic
beauties,

In their silent creaks and echoes of old,
Lie the stories of adventures, beautiful and bold.

Midnight Thoughts

You can't skip chapters, that are not of your
interest,
You have to read every line, not required to
share every secret,

You have to meet every character, as you don't
have a choice,
Some chapters make you cry for weeks, but
don't stop being nice,

You will have to go through, even if you don't
want to,
Cherish the moment when you don't want the
pages to end,

You have to keep going, as stories keep the
world revolving,
Live your own chapter, don't miss out before
you check out.

Unheard Voice

I like silence and peace,
Whether it's in Italy or Greece,
Would love to be someone's poem,
Beautifully written and composed in own
rhythm,

I like the scars 'cause I like the story,
Bravery, stupidity, pain — none of them come
free,

Want to be loved with an honest tongue,
Devoted heart and exclusive eyes,
Well, Rome took all my attention and Paris
made me realize.

Good Listener

A listener needs a listener too,
Just like the sky needs the moon,

In the quiet corners where thoughts blend,
A gentle presence, a patient friend,

Sometimes no need for words to fill space,
In silence, goodness finds its place,

They weave the threads of trust and care,
With every tale, they are always there,

A bridge of comfort, understanding and loyalty,
But it's good sometimes to check on royalty,

These factors decide how long it stands,
Here, the good listener and wisdom speaker
walk hand in hand.

Strong Arms

She is a hurricane, but pure and descent,
She is a ray of light, but beautiful & bright,
She blooms wild and shines like stars at night,
She is a lightning bolt, hence, don't accept the
blame without any fault,
She is the crisp morning air, with strong arms
that never tire,
Above all, sometimes she wanted to hold and
protect, to bend and mend,
In search of strength that guides and will defend.

The Old Trunk

In a corner of a turret room,
Where time has whispered and flowers bloom
An old trunk stands with weathered grace,
Its surface carved by nature's trace,
Once it holds a treasure trove,
Of stories that the wind wove,
Its wood now worn, its color faint,
A silent witness to the past's restraint,
The knots and cracks, like lines of age,
Hold secrets in their silent stage,
As seasons change and time moves on,
The old trunk rests from dusk till dawn,
Let us cherish what it holds,
The timeless tales that it unfolds,
For in the old trunk's steadfast core,
We find the past & so much more.

Beautiful Lie

It is told, that the word "pretty" is a skin,
Deep six-letter prison they put you in,
They say, "If you lost some weight, you'd be so
pretty",
They say, "If your skin was clearer, you'd be so
pretty",
But what they really mean is, "If only you
looked alluring, captivating, then you'd be
pretty",
Let me tell you the truth: "Beauty lies in the
eyes of beholder not on the face of the partaker",
You see, "pretty" is too small and simple a word
to capture,
The exquisitely complex human phenomenon
you are,
Every atom of yours was plucked in the quiet
cosmic moments between supernovas and stars,

A precisely chosen palette of your skin, your
eyes, your bones, from sunrise, sunsets and
skies,
So, when anybody wants to tell you how pretty
you could be,
Cut them off, stay strong, be independent,
believe in yourself, that's all you can and you
could be….

January & December

Being the two coldest months of the year,
One in the beginning, another in the end of the
year,
January takes 335 days to reach December,
But December takes 60 seconds to fall into a
new year,
One brings hopes, dreams, and resolutions,
Another one is a season of festivities, time to say
goodbye with lots of love and emotions,
December is the month of reaffirmation,
Whereas January is full of planning and
calculation,
Both are known for extreme winters,
Still January's dawn, so crisp and clear,
Beckons hope and casts away fear.

If it was that easy

I would tear it, if it was a piece of paper,
I would break it, if it was a glass bottle,
I would speak up, if it was that easy to listen,
I would feel blank, if it was captured in my
mind,
I would stay forever, if it was meant to be,
I would try again, if there was still a silver
lining,
I would never give up, if it was that easy.

Once Again

Live for 6 a.m. sunrise and 6 p.m. sunset,
Live for road trips and bike rides,
Live for rain dance, don't just get wet,
Live for ginger tea instead of American
Espresso,
Live for theater, stop being dramatic,
Live for the trek to mountain, at highest peak,
Live for deep-sea diving to feel alive,
Live for the dreams that don't let you sleep.

Unpaid Therapist

These people are stars in the night sky,
Like silver linings when all hope die,
In laughter and tears, they stand by
With hearts open, where no need to lie,
Through ups and downs, they never bend,
A constant light, a faithful friend,
In every moment, doesn't matter near or far,
They play an unpaid therapist, in love or war.

When Sun kissed the Sea

A rare beauty, beyond comparison, when sun
kissed the sea,
No scene so calm, the best equation, when sun
melts into the sea,
Dancing light on salty spray,
Seems nature is breathing, the perfect day,
As the day meets evening's glow,
Together they create a flow,
With each wave's crash, a story unfolds,
Of distant lands and treasures untold.

The Last Chapter

In the quiet dusk, the pages turn,
Whispers of journeys, lessons learned,
With every line, a life unfolds,
Laughter and secrets, dreams intertwined,
With this turning, the two hearts aligned,
With bittersweet smiles, let's stand together,
Through trials and triumphs, the bond gets
stronger.

www.ingramcontent.com/pod-product-compliance
Lightning Source LLC
LaVergne TN
LVHW041244200726
843507LV00013B/2809